Noah and the Ark

Noah and the Ark

words by Jessica d'Este
illustrations Ian Pentney

Once upon awhile ago
A Camel and a Cow
Creatures in the story
Of where and when and how

Found themselves at dancing
Adrift and dry in pairs
Afloat with Noah's family
Not going anywhere.

As it is not to be imagined
That on the occasion that they met
They were taking China tea and cake
Devon cream and crumpet.

Indeed! What is imagined?
What strange Catastrophe
That Camel, Cow and Noah
Share a Destiny?

As sand is home to Camel
And Cows, I know, eat grass
Why afloat and drifting
One is bound to ask?

The clue is: God is Goodness
And there's Sin and Death in Man
But where there's Retribution
Salvation's also planned.

God, 'tis true, allowed a flood
But, mercifully, at least
Saved one good man, his family
And two of every beast.

So to say: God said to Noah:
Build an Ark as wide
As long and deep as safely
As may huddle there inside

Tame and wild, all animals
All your family, all your goats
And any late provisions
As may happen not to float.

Whereupon the Deluge came
And Camel, Cow and all
Had forty days to contemplate
Creation and The Fall.

Forty days and nights it rained
Incessant rain came down
Inconvenient surely so
But the message is profound

Because it came to pass, a Dove
In search of land was found
Returning with an olive branch
With cries of: Water's down!

And as the water drained away
Everybody knew
Never again the Earth in flood
Would ever again God do

Because he said so there and then
With promises of Peace
Good cause for Celebration
For Woman, Man and Beast.

And so it came to be about
A party no one missed
Cow and Camel first up to dance
And for everyone a Kiss

With Joy for all and all around
Songs of Praise and Mirth
For Earth in bloom and fruit again
And all pairs giving birth.

And so the Arc, it, too, turned up
Upside down! – it seemed
As beautiful a Rainbow
As ever in a Dream –

Though the risk of Sin remains
As in the wind 'tis heard:
The fire next time, Brother!
God's given us His Word.

Limited edtion of 100 copies
signed by the poet and
the illustrator

number 57/100

Published in 2018 by Impress

Impress
Editorial Department [156]
95 Wilton Road
London, sw1v 1bz

Copyright – 2018.
All rights reserved.

No part of this publication may be reproduced, transmitted, or stored in a retrieval system, in any form, or by any means, without permission in writing from the author. This book is sold subject to the condition that it shall not, by way of trade or otherwise, be lent, hired out, resold, or otherwise circulated without the author's prior consent in any form of binding or cover other than that in which it is published, and without a similar condition being imposed on the subsequent purchaser.

Copyright restrictions in favour of the artist & poet apply. © 2018

The moral rights of the artist & poet have been asserted.

isbn 978 0 9955540 9 2

www.impress-publishing.com

Designed by Prof. Phil Cleaver
and George Gallagher
of et al design consultants.
Typeset in Monotype Albertus Nova
Print production by Dave Davies
of DLM Creative.
Printed in England by Hartgraph.